I0459149

KHALIF M. TOWNES

Built To Keep Moving

By Any Means Necessary

IMPETUS
PUBLISHING

This book is lovingly dedicated to my grandmother, Delores Warner — Grandma, you always reminded me: "When life gives you lemons, make lemonade." Those words have carried me through storms, setbacks, and seasons I thought I couldn't survive. I learned resilience. Because of you, I found the strength to keep going. Because of you, I know without question that I am BUILT TO KEEP MOVING. Your wisdom is my foundation, and your love is the push that keeps me pressing forward.

Love ya Butchy Boy!

Contents

Preface   iii

Acknowledgments   v

Introduction   1

I   When the Room Empties

1   WHEN THE CROWD CLEARS   5
2   THE SEASON OF SEPARATION   10
3   LETDOWNS & LESSONS   16
4   SQUARE ONE, BUT WISER   22

II   The Shift Requires Sacrifice

5   THE GRIT OF DESPERATION   29
6   EARLY MORNINGS & LATE NIGHTS   35
7   WHEN RESOURCES RUN LOW   41
8   THE POWER OF FOCUSED ISOLATION   48

III   By Any Means Necessary

9   CARRYING YOUR OWN VISION   59
10   BUILT TO KEEP MOVING   66
11   YOUR MOMENTUM IS YOUR MIRACLE   73

12 THE BREAKTHROUGH ON THE OTHER
     SIDE OF GRIT   80

Afterword   85
Declarations for the Determined   89

Preface

Life has a way of testing the very core of who we are. Not just through the victories we celebrate but through the valleys we barely survive. I didn't write this book from a mountaintop; I wrote it from the trenches—moments when quitting seemed easier, when disappointment felt heavier than hope, and when silence from the very people I expected to lean on almost crushed me.

But what I discovered along the way is this: being "built to keep moving" isn't about avoiding obstacles—it's about surviving them. It's about pushing forward when strength is gone, trusting God when clarity is cloudy, and believing there's more ahead even when everything around you says "stop here."

This book isn't just my story—it's a mirror. As you turn these pages, you may see pieces of your own journey. My prayer is that you find encouragement for the moments you almost gave up, strategies for the seasons when vision felt blurry, and fire for the days when you need to remind yourself you were built for this.

If nothing else, let this preface prepare you: this is not a book about comfort—it's a book about courage. It's a reminder that even when the room empties, when support fades, when sacrifice feels costly, you have everything you need to keep moving. And when you do, you'll see that every tear, every trial, and every test was only proof of what you were made of.

Because you weren't just created—you were built.
And you were built to keep moving.

Acknowledgments

First and foremost, I thank God. It is only by His grace, wisdom, and unfailing love that I am able to stand, create, and fulfill purpose. Every idea, every word, and every opportunity comes from Him, and to Him belongs all the glory.

I honor my mother and father—thank you for being you! without you two, it would be no me.

To my friends and family who pushed me when I wanted to give up, and reminded me of who I am when I doubted myself—your encouragement has been fuel in seasons when I needed it most. I am deeply grateful for your belief in me.

A special acknowledgment to my Spiritual Mother, Dr. Valerie Moore. Thank you for your impartation, your prayers, your teaching, and the wisdom you've poured into me. Your covering and guidance have been a constant source of strength and clarity.

And finally, to every reader of this book—thank you for walking this journey with me. My prayer is that these words serve as a reminder that vision is possible, destiny is real, and with faith, persistence, and God's timing, manifestation always comes.

Acknowledgments

Introduction

There comes a moment in life when you look around for the people you thought you needed—and they're gone. The ones you were sure would stand by your side in this next season are suddenly silent. The ones you trusted with your dreams, your vision, and your heart have disappeared. And the sting isn't just in their absence; it's in the fact that you were counting on them. You waited and waited, thinking, "Any day now they'll show up. Any day now they'll step in." But the truth? They didn't. And the longer you waited, the more you realized—they're not coming.

When that reality hits, you've got two choices: you can stop and cry over who's not here, or you can get up and move forward by any means necessary. For me, it wasn't just about people leaving—it was about what their absence revealed. I quickly learned that there are seasons in life when the shift you're experiencing isn't meant for everyone to be a part of—not even friends, not even family. As much as you want to take certain people with you, God has a way of clearing the room so the next chapter unfolds exactly how it's supposed to.

And let me be honest—this isn't a clean, Instagram-worthy process. Sometimes it looks like early mornings and late nights. Sometimes it means doing the work you thought would be split among three people, all by yourself. Sometimes it means going back to square one, not because you failed, but because you're rebuilding with different hands this time—your own. When resources start running low and your support circle is nonexistent, you discover something powerful: either you stop, or you rise.

And when you decide to rise, something shifts inside you. It's that "If I have to do it all myself, I'm still going to make it happen" kind of determination. It's a quiet, stubborn, unshakable decision that says, "This vision will live—with or without help." That's what *Built to Keep Moving* is all about. It's not just a book— it's a declaration. It's for anyone who's ever been left holding the pieces of their dream, wondering if they have the strength to keep going. It's for the person rebuilding from the ground up, the one working with limited resources but unlimited faith. It's for the person whose back is against the wall and still finds a way to push forward.

This book will walk you through what I've learned in these seasons—not from a place of theory, but from the trenches. We'll talk about how to keep moving when the people you counted on vanish, how to turn separation into strength, how to push when you're tired, broke, and seemingly alone, and how to tap into the resilience that's already in you. By the time you reach the last page, I want you to feel that same fire I felt when I realized: no matter who walks away, no matter what dries up, no matter how heavy it feels—you are built to keep moving, by any means necessary.

Let's get to work.

—Khalif M. Townes

I

When the Room Empties

When the room empties, the silence can feel louder than the applause ever did. You look around and realize the crowd that once cheered has moved on, the hands that once helped have let go. It stings, but it's also revealing. Empty rooms strip away false support and show you who you really are when no one's watching. And in that quiet, you find a strength you didn't know you carried — the kind that doesn't need a crowd to keep moving forward.

1

WHEN THE CROWD CLEARS

There's a peculiar quietness that settles in once the excitement fades. When you're pursuing a dream, launching a vision, or entering a new season, the beginning is usually filled with energy. People applaud, cheer, and promise to stand by you "no matter what." They share your posts, express their pride, and offer their help with phrases like, "Just call me if you need anything."

BUT THEN THE CROWD DISPERSES

You begin to notice the **empty spaces where you expected familiar faces**. The people you thought would be front and center have vanished. Some withdrew quietly. Some stopped returning calls. Some left without explanation.

Initially, it feels personal. *What did I do wrong? Why did they disappear? Did I say something? Was I not enough?*

You analyze past conversations, dissecting every interaction, searching for ways to fix it.

But here's what I've learned: Sometimes the crowd doesn't

clear because you failed. Sometimes it clears because **the next part of your journey isn't meant to be a group project**.

THE REALITY OF BEING ALONE

When I first entered this season, I thought something was broken. The people I had relied on for years — those who promised to be there through everything — were suddenly absent. It felt like more than a shift; it felt like betrayal.

But the longer I sat with the silence, the more I understood: **This wasn't punishment. It was positioning & strategy**.

Being alone forced me to discover what I was truly made of. Without a safety net, you move differently. You stop waiting for someone to catch you and learn to land on your own feet. When there's no backup plan, you tap into a deeper level of grit — the kind you didn't know existed until the weight was entirely on your shoulders.

When "we" becomes "me," you stop seeking permission or applause and realize you were equipped to carry this vision all along.

Aloneness is uncomfortable, but it's also clarifying. It reveals who you are without the noise, without the crowd, without the crutch of constant validation. And in that stillness, you begin to see — maybe you weren't supposed to have that safety net in this season. Maybe the only way to step fully into what's next was to walk it alone, so that when you arrive, you'll know **it was you and God who got you there**.

THE BLESSING OF THE EMPTY ROOM

It took time to understand that God wasn't subtracting from my life — He was making space.

When the room started to clear, I thought I was losing. The people I laughed with, planned with, and leaned on were gone. At first, I tried to hold on — to call them back into the room. But no matter what I did, they didn't return.

I didn't know then that the empty chairs were intentional.

Some people can't go with you because they would dilute your next level — watering down what God is about to pour in. Some can't go because they aren't willing to stretch the way you have to stretch. They'd rather stay comfortable while **you're called to climb**. And some can't go because their assignment in your life was tied to the last season, not the next one. Their role was complete, even if it didn't feel like it.

It hurts when familiar faces fade. It's lonely when the voices you counted on go silent. But here's the blessing: when the room empties, the noise quiets. And in that quiet, you're no longer distracted by voices that were never meant to guide you into your future.

You can hear God more clearly. You can see your own strength more vividly. You start to realize **the empty room isn't a loss — it's a sacred space**, cleared and prepared for what's about to be birthed in you.

WHAT TO DO WHEN THE CROWD CLEARS

The quiet can feel like a void — like something's missing. But it's often the very space you need to think clearly, hear God's voice, and move without distraction.

When the noise fades and the room empties, here's what to hold onto:

1. **Don't Beg People to Stay** If someone was meant to walk into the next chapter of your story, they'd still be here. Begging them to stay only keeps you tied to a season that has already ended. Let them go with grace, and trust that God knows exactly who needs to be in your life for what's ahead.

2. **Resist the Urge to Pause Your Progress** It's tempting to stop moving when it feels like you've been left alone. But progress isn't always fast — sometimes it's one small step at a time. Even slow movement is better than standing still. Keep going, even if all you can manage is a single step each day.

3. **Use the Silence to Strategize** Fewer voices mean fewer distractions. Use this time to plan, to dream, and to listen. Let God download the next instructions without them being filtered through other people's opinions or fears. Quiet seasons are fertile ground for clarity.

4. **Lean Into Your Own Capacity** This is when you find out what you're truly made of. You'll surprise yourself with the ideas, solutions, and strength that rise up when you have no choice but to rely on what God has already placed in you. What feels like lack is often hidden potential waiting to be activated.

MY OWN TURNING POINT

I remember sitting at my desk one night, looking at a list of tasks I had expected three people to help me with — and realizing it was all on me now.

It was overwhelming. I felt abandoned. Felt like what the heck was I even thinking.

But then something rose up in me: *If I've got to do it all myself, then I'm going to do it!*

That decision changed everything.

I stopped waiting for people to validate me. I stopped wishing for the "old crew" to come back. I started building — one long night, one early morning, one quiet breakthrough at a time.

The crowd clearing isn't the end of your story. It's the start of a chapter where you get to see exactly what you're made of. And when you keep moving in this season, you're not just proving people wrong... You're proving to yourself that **you were built for this**.

* * *

Reflection: Think of one area in your life right now where you feel abandoned or unsupported. Ask yourself: If I stopped waiting for help and started today with what I have, what's the first move I could make? Write it down — and do it.

Declaration: "I am not afraid of the empty room. I will not be paralyzed by who left. I am built to keep moving, even if it's just me and God. I will move forward by any means necessary."

2

THE SEASON OF SEPARATION

NOT EVERYONE CAN GO WHERE YOU'RE GOING

The truth about moving into your next season is this: **IT'S NOT FOR EVERYBODY!**

That's one of the hardest truths to accept.

You can love people deeply, value their presence, and genuinely want them to share in the fruit of your next chapter... but that doesn't mean they're supposed to be there.

You imagine the celebration. You picture the same people who were there at the start, standing beside you at the finish. You dream of crossing the line together.

But sometimes, stepping into what's next triggers a separation you never asked for — and one you never saw coming.

It's not always dramatic. Sometimes it's quiet — a slow drift, a missed call here, an unanswered message there. Other times, it's sharp and sudden, like a door slamming shut.

And while your heart may want to fight for their place in your future, your spirit will eventually recognize the truth:

Not everyone can handle where you're going. Not everyone can carry the weight of your next. Not everyone is called to climb the same mountain you're called to scale.

WHY SEPARATION HAPPENS

I used to think people leaving meant I had failed them somehow. I thought it was about my shortcomings, my mistakes, or something I could've done differently.

But over time, I've learned that separation is often divine strategy. God is making room, not creating loss.

Here's what I've discovered:

- **Different Callings Require Different Capacities** – Your next season will demand a level of discipline, faith, and sacrifice that not everyone is willing to give.

- **Hidden Motives Get Exposed** – Some people clap for you as long as your success doesn't surpass their comfort zone. The closer you get to breakthrough, the more their real intentions surface.

- **Dead Weight Slows the Climb** – Carrying people who aren't built for the journey will drain your energy before you reach the summit. God loves you too much to let that happen.

Separation doesn't always mean the other person is "bad." It means **their role in your story has ended** — and that's okay.

THE PAIN BEFORE THE CLARITY

Let's be honest — separation hurts.

It can feel like rejection, even when it's really redirection. You remember the laughs you shared, the battles you fought together, the dreams you dreamed out loud. And it's natural to want to go back.

But going back to keep someone in your life can cost you the very thing God is trying to give you.

I've learned this: when God closes a door on certain relationships, **it's never to punish you — it's to protect you**.

If you try to drag people from your past into your future, you'll eventually discover **they can't breathe in the altitude you're called to**.

SIGNS YOU'RE IN A SEASON OF SEPARATION

Sometimes you can feel something shifting before you can put words to it. You just know the connection doesn't feel the same. If you're wondering whether you're in this season, pay attention to these signs:

1. **Unexplainable Distance** – People you once talked to every day now feel far away. They're "too busy," unavailable, or slow to respond, and no matter how much you try to bridge the gap, it stays there.

2. **Shifting Conversations** – The things that used to spark mutual excitement now fall flat. You share your vision and get silence, skepticism, or a quick change of subject. They're no longer speaking the same language as your

destiny.

3. **Misaligned Energy** – You walk away from time spent together feeling heavy, drained, or discouraged instead of inspired and fueled. Their presence takes more from you than it gives.

4. **Closed Doors** – The opportunities that used to flow through certain connections have slowed down or stopped altogether. The pathways you once relied on are no longer open — and forcing them feels wrong.

These aren't random. These aren't coincidences. They're clues — gentle (and sometimes not-so-gentle) hints from God that **the season is shifting, and certain connections can't go where you're headed**.

CHOOSING TO LET GO

Letting go doesn't mean you don't care. It doesn't mean you've given up on people. And it certainly doesn't mean you've failed.

Letting go is an act of wisdom. It's a choice to protect your pace, your peace, and your purpose.

It's saying: "I honor what we shared, but **I refuse to lose my momentum pulling you into something you're not called to** — and may not even want to be part of."

When you **release with peace**, you're not just removing someone from your journey — you're making room for what is meant to walk alongside you. You create space for the right voices, the right resources, and the right opportunities to find you.

It's not about bitterness. It's about alignment. It's not about burning bridges. It's about building boundaries.

Because the truth is, **carrying the wrong weight will keep you from reaching the right destination**.

MY OWN SEPARATION STORY

I can't tell you how many times I slowed my own pace, thinking I was being loyal.

I told myself, "They just need more time. We'll grow together. Eventually, they'll see the vision the way I see it."

I waited. And in waiting, I lost time. I lost energy. I lost opportunities that would never come back around in the same way.

I was holding myself hostage to the hope that everyone I started with would finish with me. But the truth was, not everyone had the capacity, the calling, or the desire to run at the same speed.

It wasn't until I embraced the separation that my pace picked up.

And here's the part that surprised me — **some of my greatest breakthroughs came after the room got smaller**.

When the distractions disappeared, so did the noise. When the opinions faded, so did the confusion. What I was left with was more focus... and more progress.

The smaller the circle, the clearer the vision. The clearer the vision, the faster the movement.

The Season of Separation isn't punishment — it's preparation. It's not God taking something from you; it's Him getting you ready for something greater. He's lightening your load so you can climb higher without breaking under the weight.

He's removing the distractions so you can hear His instructions clearly. He's clearing the path so that when you step into the next season, you'll have the strength, focus, and freedom to run at full speed.

And the faster you accept that, the lighter and faster you'll move. **Your energy will shift from chasing people to chasing purpose. Your focus will turn from who left to what's next. Your heart will trade grief for gratitude**.

Because when you finally see what God was preparing you for, you'll realize the separation wasn't just necessary — it was a gift.

* * *

Reflection: Identify one person, situation, or commitment you've been holding onto that no longer aligns with where you're going. Ask yourself: Am I keeping this out of loyalty... or out of fear of being alone?

Declaration: "I trust the process of separation. I release who and what no longer serves my next season. I refuse to carry weight that God never intended for me to bear. I am free to move forward by any means necessary."

3

LETDOWNS & LESSONS

THE REALITY OF DISAPPOINTMENT

If you live long enough, you're going to face disappointment. It's not a matter of if — it's only a matter of when.

And the thing about disappointment is, it rarely sends a warning. It doesn't knock on your door politely and give you time to prepare. **It hits suddenly** — sometimes with a quiet sting, sometimes with the force of a punch you never saw coming.

We love to talk about the lessons that come from success — the moments where everything lines up and the reward feels worth the work. But the truth is, some of the most valuable wisdom you will ever gain won't come from the wins... it will be born out of the letdowns.

Because **disappointment has a way of pulling the mask off reality**. It reveals who's really committed and who was just convenient. It tests whether your belief in the vision was strong enough to survive a blow. And it forces you to decide — will you stop here, or will you use this pain as fuel?

THE GUT PUNCH OF BEING LET DOWN

Letdowns cut deep because they live in the gap between what you expected and what actually happened.

You trusted someone. You believed their word. You invested your time, your energy, and sometimes even your heart and money into the idea that they would come through.

And then — they didn't.

The silence after the promise stings. The cancellation after the commitment stings. The excuse that comes when they should have just been honest stings.

Sometimes it's betrayal — intentional, sharp, and personal. Sometimes it's negligence — they simply didn't care enough to follow through. Sometimes it's **people overpromising and underdelivering** — trying to impress you in the moment but unable to sustain it when it counted.

Whatever the cause, the hurt is real. It doesn't just bruise your feelings — it shakes your trust, makes you question your discernment, and forces you to confront the uncomfortable truth that not everyone values commitment the way you do.

But here's the other truth: That sting can either become the wound that stops you... or the lesson that strengthens you.

MY TURNING POINT WITH DISAPPOINTMENT

There was a moment in my journey when I had built my plans around someone else's role in my vision. A few people if I'm totally honest.

Not just loosely — I was counting on them. Their effort. Their skills. Their commitment. I had made room for them, believing they were not only willing but ready.

And then, at the exact point I needed them most... they backed out.

It wasn't just inconvenient. It felt personal.

I had shifted my life, my schedule, and my energy to include them in the process. In one instant, I went from confident planning to scrambling for a solution.

At first, I was frustrated. Then I was hurt. Then, honestly, I was tempted to quit.

Because **disappointment doesn't just bruise your feelings — it messes with your trust**. It makes you second-guess your instincts, your decisions, even your calling.

But in that moment, I realized I had a choice. I could camp in the pain of the letdown... replaying it until it robbed me of my momentum. Or I could mine it for the lesson — the insight, the wisdom, the clarity that only comes when life forces you to see things for what they really are.

That day, I chose the lesson. And that choice changed everything.

THE LESSON IN EVERY LETDOWN

Disappointment has a way of feeling like a thief. It sneaks in and steals your hope, your joy, and your expectations. But if you pay attention, it can also be one of your greatest teachers.

Here's what I've learned disappointment will teach you — if you let it:

1. **People's Commitment Has an Expiration Date** Not everyone is meant to stay for the entire journey. Some were only assigned to a chapter, not the whole book. When you understand this, you stop taking their exit so personally.

18

2. **Your Vision Must Be Bigger Than Any One Person** If your dream falls apart when one person walks away, it wasn't built solid enough. Disappointment forces you to fortify your vision so it stands — even if you're standing alone.

3. **The Backup Plan is You** Disappointment shows you that waiting for someone to save the day isn't an option. You are the plan. Your resilience is the safety net.

4. **Closed Doors Can Be Divine Protection** Sometimes God allows people to pull away because their presence would slow your progress or compromise your next level. What feels like rejection is often redirection.

5. **Pain Can Produce Precision** After being let down, you become more intentional about who you trust, how you plan, and where you invest your energy. Disappointment sharpens your discernment.

The sting may still hurt, but the wisdom you gain will outlast the wound.

TURNING PAIN INTO FUEL

One of the most powerful decisions you can ever make is to turn disappointment into determination.

Instead of replaying the scene in your head and saying, "I can't believe they let me down," flip the script and declare, "I can't believe I almost let this stop me."

Every letdown is proof of movement. It means you're still in motion. It means the vision is still alive and worth fighting for.

The sting you feel... That's evidence that you care. And **if you care enough to feel the pain, you should care enough to finish the work**.

Pain can either paralyze you or propel you. The choice is yours. And when you choose propulsion over paralysis, disappointment becomes fuel for your next breakthrough.

Here's the hidden blessing: every time someone doesn't show up for you, you get the opportunity to show up for yourself in a brand-new way. You start finding solutions you didn't think you had. You develop resilience you didn't know you possessed. You prove — to yourself — that **your calling is not dependent on someone else's consistency**.

The truth is, letdowns are crossroads. They can stop you dead in your tracks, or they can become the very moments that forge you into someone unshakable.

The difference is in the choice you make after the sting fades: Will you camp out in disappointment? Or will you rise from it with more grit, more clarity, and more determination than ever before?

* * *

Reflection: Think back to the last time someone let you down. Write out what you learned from it. Then write one way you can apply that lesson to your current season so you move forward stronger.

Declaration: "I will not let disappointment derail my destiny. I will extract the lesson, apply the wisdom, and keep moving forward by any means necessary."

4

SQUARE ONE, BUT WISER

STARTING OVER ISN'T STARTING FROM SCRATCH

Starting over can feel like defeat — until you realize what you're really standing on this time.

When life, business, or relationships fall apart, it's tempting to look at the wreckage and think, "Here I am again, right back where I started."

But the truth is, you're not starting from scratch. You're starting from experience — and that's the difference between rebuilding and repeating.

This time, **you're armed with lessons that cost you something to learn**. This time, you know the pitfalls before you step into them. This time, you've got **wisdom that only comes from walking through what tried to break you**.

So don't discount the ground you're standing on. It's not the same place — it's higher ground.

THE MYTH OF SQUARE ONE

We call it "square one" because it feels like the beginning all over again. But this isn't the same starting line you faced years ago.

Back then, you were fueled mostly by excitement. Now, you're fueled by hard-earned wisdom.

Back then, you were guessing your way forward. Now, you've got a map made of every wrong turn, closed door, and painful lesson.

The game has changed because you've changed.

WHAT MAKES YOU WISER NOW

When life pushes you to rebuild, you don't return to the table as the same person who started. You walk in with battle scars that have sharpened your instincts.

- **Sharper Discernment** – You've learned to spot red flags before they become roadblocks.

- **Better Boundaries** – You now know who can be trusted — and exactly how far.

- **Greater Efficiency** – You've discovered what drains you and what actually moves you forward.

- **More Grit** – You've weathered letdowns, survived separations, and pushed through nights when quitting felt easier.

The beauty of this moment is that you're not building blindly anymore. You're laying your foundation with precision, using the wisdom bought with every tear, every "no," and every closed door.

And because of that, this rebuild isn't just about getting back what was lost — it's about constructing something stronger than you ever had before.

MY SQUARE ONE MOMENT

I'll never forget the day it hit me — I was back at square one.

The people I had planned with were gone. The partnerships I invested in had dissolved. My carefully crafted timeline had vanished in weeks.

At first, it felt like failure all over again. I caught myself asking, "How am I back here?"

But then something clicked.

This wasn't the same "square one" I faced years ago. Back then, my stomach was in knots, my head was full of doubt, and I had no idea if I'd make it.

This time, I wasn't afraid.

Because I had proof. Proof that I could build from nothing. Proof that I could recover from loss. Proof that I could turn a setback into a setup.

The frustration was real, but so was the confidence. And that's when I realized — **starting over isn't the same when you've already survived it once.**

THE ADVANTAGE OF A SECOND START

The hidden blessing of finding yourself back at "square one" is this: you get to build right this time.

No more rushing past red flags. No more investing in the wrong people. No more chasing opportunities that pull you away from your purpose.

This time, you're intentional. Every move is measured. Every decision is backed by both clarity and conviction.

You're not building from the same place you started before — you're building from experience. And that experience has given you a steady hand, a sharper eye, and a stronger backbone.

Because you've already survived a fall, you walk differently into the rebuild. **You're not tentative — you're purposeful. You're not desperate — you're discerning**.

The beauty of a second start isn't just that you get another chance. It's that you know exactly what to do with it.

BUILDING WITHOUT THE BAGGAGE

One of the greatest shifts you can make in this season is learning to build without dragging the past into every new decision.

Your past holds lessons, yes — but it was never meant to be the blueprint for your future. If you use it as a guide for wisdom, it will sharpen you. If you use it as a chain, it will slow you down.

The key is in the balance:

- **Keep the wisdom** — the discernment, the boundaries, the clarity you've earned.

- **Release the weight** — the resentment, the fear, the over-thinking that keeps you playing small.

When you stop treating every new opportunity like it's guilty until proven innocent, you create space for fresh vision and fresh momentum.

That's how you turn "square one" into "level two" — by showing up lighter, clearer, and ready to build something stronger without the shadows of what broke before.

The truth is, starting over isn't a setback — it's a setup. You're not weaker because you had to rebuild. You're stronger because you chose to.

* * *

Reflection: Think about an area in your life where you've had to start over. Write down three lessons from your last attempt that you can use to build stronger this time.

Declaration: "I am not starting over empty. I am starting over equipped. Every lesson I've learned will work for me in this next season. I am wiser, stronger, and built to keep moving by any means necessary."

II

The Shift Requires Sacrifice

*The shift requires sacrifice — not because you're
being punished, but because you're being prepared.
Every elevation demands that something be left
behind: old habits, draining relationships, or the
comfort of "how it's always been." Sacrifice stings
because it feels like loss, but it's really an exchange.
You're trading what can't sustain you for what will
carry you into your next. The shift will cost you, yes —
but what you gain on the other side will prove it was
worth every sacrifice.*

5

THE GRIT OF DESPERATION

WHEN DESPERATION BECOMES YOUR WEAPON

Desperation has a way of stripping away the fluff. It silences excuses. It exposes the difference between wanting something and needing it.

When you're desperate enough, you stop looking for perfect timing because you realize perfect timing isn't coming. You stop waiting for every piece to line up because you know life doesn't work that way. You stop saying, "When I feel ready," because you accept that readiness is a decision, not a feeling.

In desperation, later becomes now. Not because it's comfortable. Not because you're confident. But because you've run out of options — and that's when you find out what you're really made of.

Desperation turns hesitation into movement. It turns "maybe" into "must." And it teaches you that the gritty, imperfect step you take today is worth more than the flawless plan you never execute.

DESPERATION ISN'T ALWAYS A BAD THING

We hear the word desperate and immediately picture panic, weakness, or hopelessness. But that's only half the story.

In the right hands, desperation is a weapon. It's a spark that ignites movement when comfort would have kept you stuck. It's a jolt that wakes you from the lull of "I'll get to it" and shoves you into now.

Desperation sharpens focus. It strips away distractions. It makes you stop asking "Should I?" and start declaring "I must."

It's the force that makes you dig deeper when you've already given everything you thought you had. It's the moment you stop negotiating with your dream and draw a line in the sand: *This has to happen. I don't have another option.*

Desperation, when channeled, doesn't make you weaker — it makes you unstoppable.

THE GRIT IT UNLOCKS

Grit is that mental toughness that says, "I'll keep going no matter what." But grit rarely shows up uninvited. It's not born in the comfort of abundance — it's forged in the fire of desperation.

When the bills are due and there's no backup plan. When the clock is ticking louder than your own heartbeat. When the resources are gone. When the people you thought you could count on have disappeared. And all that's left... is you, your vision, and the faith that if you take the next step, God will meet you there.

That's when grit rises.

It's the quiet voice that tells you, "**Get up, keep moving, don't**

you dare stop here." It's the fuel that pushes you into motion even when your body is tired and your mind is screaming for an easier way.

Grit will have you doing what you once thought was impossible:

- Waking up before the sun because you know the early hours are sacred.

- Working deep into the night because this moment can't be wasted.

- Learning skills you swore you could never master because you refuse to wait on someone else to save your vision.

Desperation may light the fire — but grit is what keeps it burning until you see the breakthrough.

MY OWN GRIT SEASON

There was a time I had no choice but to keep moving — even when my tank was bone dry.

Every ounce of energy had been spent. Every plan I thought was secure had crumbled. The people I believed would help carry the weight... **GONE.** The funding I was counting on to push things forward? Delayed. Nowhere in sight.

I sat there in the quiet, staring at the reality in front of me, and the thought hit me hard: "If I stop now, everything I've bled for, prayed for, and fought for... dies here."

That thought alone lit something inside me that no pep talk could spark.

31

I didn't have the team. I didn't have the cushion. But I had grit — and when grit is all you've got left, you find out it can take you places talent alone never could.

Grit is stubborn faith in motion. It doesn't wait for ideal conditions. It doesn't need applause or backup to move forward. It just refuses to die until the mission is complete.

THE BEAUTY OF THE PRESSURE COOKER

Desperation has a way of dropping you into a pressure cooker. It's hot. It's tight. It's uncomfortable. And yet, it's exactly the environment where raw potential becomes something refined and powerful.

The heat of pressure does three undeniable things:

- **It burns away the distractions.** Suddenly, the things that used to consume your time don't matter. Only what moves you forward survives.

- **It demands immediate action.** There's no room for "later." The clock becomes your coach, and urgency becomes your discipline.

- **It pulls out hidden resourcefulness.** You start finding solutions in places you never thought to look. You discover ideas, skills, and boldness you didn't know you had.

What began as "I'm running out of time" shifted into "I'm about to make the most of every second I have."

Because under pressure, you don't just survive — you transform.

HARNESSING DESPERATION WITHOUT LETTING IT BREAK YOU

Desperation is a powerful fuel — but like any fuel, it burns hot. If you don't manage it, it will scorch you before you ever reach the finish line.

The key is to channel that intensity into sustainable forward motion:

- **Pace Yourself.** Desperation makes you want to sprint nonstop, but every race — even the urgent ones — has to be run with strategy. Push too hard too soon, and you'll have nothing left when it matters most.

- **Honor Rest as a Weapon.** Rest isn't weakness. It's a strategic pause to recharge your mind and body so you can keep showing up with full strength. Even warriors sleep before battle.

- **Keep Your "Why" Front and Center.** In the chaos, you'll be tempted to work just for the sake of working. But desperation without direction turns into burnout. Keep your mission, your vision, and your reason for fighting in clear view — it will help you push with focus instead of just panic.

When you manage desperation, you turn it from a fire that consumes you into a fire that propels you.

When you come out of a desperation season, you don't just walk away with a victory — you walk away with weapons you didn't have before.

You'll know what it means to work under pressure, when every moment counts and hesitation could cost you everything. You'll know how to push without waiting for permission, validation, or a perfect plan. You'll know how to keep moving when every sign says it's impossible, when the odds aren't just against you — they're daring you to quit.

And most importantly, you'll know this unshakable truth: **Grit will take you places comfort never will.**

Comfort wants you to stay safe. Grit will carry you into unknown territory and make sure you come back with proof that it can be done.

* * *

Reflection: Think about a time in your life when you had no choice but to make something happen. What did that pressure teach you about yourself? Write down three strengths you discovered during that season.

Declaration: "I will not fear desperation. I will use it as fuel. My grit is unshakable, my vision is clear, and I am built to keep moving by any means necessary."

6

EARLY MORNINGS & LATE NIGHTS

When the vision sits heavy on your spirit, it changes the way you live.

It won't let you sleep the way you used to.

You wake up with it whispering in your mind before the sun even rises.

You carry it with you through the day, even when you're doing a hundred other things.

And when the world finally gets quiet at night, there it is again — reminding you that it still needs you.

Somewhere along the way, you realize:

If this dream is going to breathe, if it's going to live, you'll have to work in the hours most people give to comfort.

You'll have to rise earlier than the crowd and stay up later than the excuses.

Because birthing something big demands time that comfort will never volunteer.

WHY THIS SEASON DEMANDS MORE OF YOU

Breakthroughs don't punch a time clock.

They don't care about "business hours."

They show up in moments when you're willing to be where most won't go — and stay longer than most will stay.

Sometimes, they come before sunrise, when the air is still and the noise of the world hasn't yet found you.

Other times, they arrive well past midnight, when everyone else has shut down, and it's just you, the vision, and the glow of your screen or the scratch of your pen.

Early mornings and late nights aren't just proof that you're "working hard."

They're sacred hours — uninterrupted space where you can move the vision forward without the constant pull of notifications, phone calls, and the opinions of others.

In these hours, your thoughts have room to stretch.

Your spirit has room to listen.

You hear God's whisper without competing voices.

And what you create in those moments carries a weight and clarity that only comes when you're willing to give more than what's convenient.

THE SACRIFICE OF UNUSUAL HOURS

Let's be real — there's nothing glamorous about this part.

You're going to lose some sleep.

You'll miss a few dinners, parties, and casual nights of doing nothing.

Your phone might buzz with invites you have to decline, and yes, there will be mornings when coffee feels less like a drink and more like survival.

In all honesty— this isn't punishment.

It's a season.

And like all seasons, it will pass.

Right now, you're sowing in soil most people won't touch.

These early mornings and late nights are the dark, quiet hours when seeds go into the ground — hidden, unseen, but alive with potential.

What you're building may not look like much now, but every decision, every late-night push, every early start is a deposit toward the harvest you'll live on later.

One day, you'll wake up and realize you're living off the fruit of the very hours that once felt like sacrifice.

And when that moment comes, you'll know — **none of it was wasted**.

MY EARLY MORNING/LATE NIGHT SHIFT

There was a stretch of my life where the clock didn't belong to me — it belonged to the vision.

My days didn't end until 2:00 AM, and they started again before 6:00 AM.

It wasn't about bragging rights or proving I could survive without sleep.

It wasn't because I thought burning out was a badge of honor.

It was because I understood something with absolute clarity:

The window to build what I was called to build would not be open forever.

Opportunities have an expiration date.

Seasons shift.

Doors close.

And I refused to look back one day and realize the only thing I gave my vision was the leftover scraps of my time and energy.

So I rearranged my life.

I traded late-night TV for late-night strategy.

I replaced lazy mornings with intentional mornings.

I carved out the hours no one else could see — the ones when the world was quiet — and I filled them with nothing but progress.

Those hours were my personal investment into the future I said I wanted.

And every single one of them was worth it.

DISCIPLINE OVER MOTIVATION

The truth is, you won't always feel like getting up early or staying up late.

Your body will protest.

Your mind will bargain.

Your emotions will try to convince you that you've done "enough for today."

But in this season, **discipline must speak louder than comfort**.

Motivation is a feeling — and feelings are fickle.

Discipline is a decision — and decisions hold even when the feelings fade.

Discipline says:

- "I'll do it tired, because tired doesn't mean I'm done."
- "I'll do it even if no one notices, because results notice."
- "I'll do it now so I can rest later without regret."

This is the part of the journey where your habits become your engine.

Where your routine carries you when your passion feels like it's running on empty.

Because when this season ends, the work you put in now will speak for you — louder than any excuse ever could.

PROTECTING THE TIME

If you're going to commit to early mornings or late nights, you must guard that time like it's sacred — because **it is!**

These are not "leftover hours." They are your advantage hours — the time when distractions are low, clarity is high, and you can make progress without interruption.

That means:

- No scrolling aimlessly during your power hours — every minute is a deposit into your future.

- No saying yes to every invitation that pulls you away — you're not being rude, you're being responsible.

- No wasting the quiet on things that don't move the needle — if it doesn't bring you closer, it's in the way.

Think of these hours as your hidden edge. While others sleep, you're building. While others are catching up, you're getting ahead.

One day, the results will speak — and people will wonder how you got so far, so fast.

The answer will be simple: You protected the time everyone else gave away.

When the results start showing, people will call it luck.

They'll say you "just caught a break" or "were in the right place at the right time."

But they won't see the mornings you got up before the sun.

They won't see the nights you stayed up long after the world shut down.

They won't see you pushing through exhaustion, choosing discipline over comfort, protecting your hours like your life depended on it.

They won't see the cost — but you will.

You'll remember every hour you invested, every distraction you turned down, every sacrifice you made in silence.

And in that moment, you'll know it was worth it.

Not because the world is applauding, but because you kept your promise to yourself and gave your vision what it needed to live.

* * *

Reflection: Look at your current schedule. Where can you carve out 1-2 hours in the morning or at night that are completely dedicated to your vision? Write it down — and commit to protecting it this week.

Declaration: "I will give my vision the best of my time, not the leftovers. I will rise early, stay late, and do the work that others won't to live the life they can't. I am built to keep moving by any means necessary."

7

WHEN RESOURCES RUN LOW

Nothing tests your determination like running low on resources. It's easy to move when you have every tool, every contact, every dollar you think you need.

It's another thing entirely to keep moving when the budget is tight, the supplies are scarce, and the doors you thought would swing open are still locked shut.

That's the season when your commitment is proven.

When you find out whether you were in it for the convenience... or for the calling.

It's in this season you learn to stretch what's left.

To find a way when "no way" seems like the only option.

To turn creativity into currency and faith into forward motion.

This is where you discover that lack isn't the end — it's the forge.

It refines your vision, strips away waste, and forces you to focus only on what matters most.

And when you come out of it, you'll know without a doubt:

You can build even in the lean seasons... because your drive was never dependent on abundance.

THE REALITY CHECK OF SCARCITY

Running low forces you to face a hard question:

Do I want this bad enough to keep going without all the pieces in place?

A lot of people stop right here.

They tell themselves, "I'll start again when the money comes in," or "I'll wait until I can afford everything I need."

But truth be told — if you stop every time resources get thin, you'll never finish.

Scarcity doesn't mean stop.

It means shift.

Shift your perspective.

Shift your strategy.

Shift your use of what's already in your hands.

Scarcity has a way of stripping away the unnecessary and revealing just how much you can do with far less than you thought.

It forces you into innovation.

It demands that you trade excuses for execution.

When you stop seeing scarcity as a dead end and start treating it like a proving ground, you'll realize — the lack didn't block you.

It built you.

SCARCITY AS A CATALYST

Here's the secret:

Some of my most creative, breakthrough ideas weren't born in abundance — they were created in the tightest seasons, when my resources were at rock bottom.

When you can't buy your way to a solution, you start building your way there.

When you can't outsource the work, you roll up your sleeves and learn the skill yourself.

When you can't afford "top of the line," you make the most of what's already in your hands — and somehow, it's enough.

Scarcity has a way of stripping away the fluff and forcing you to focus on what truly matters.

It pushes you to innovate.

It demands that you prioritize.

It compels you to maximize every single ounce of what you've got.

The irony?

You may think scarcity is your disadvantage, but in reality — it's often the very thing that develops the creativity, resilience, and grit that abundance never could.

MY LOWEST RESOURCE SEASON

I've had seasons where the budget was so tight, I didn't just wonder how I was going to keep things afloat — I was staring at the numbers knowing they didn't add up.

The math said it was impossible.

Logic said it was time to shut it down.

And honestly?

For a moment, I almost did.

But right in the middle of that pressure, I asked myself a simple question that changed everything:

"What can I do with what I have right now?"

That question shifted me from panic to problem-solving.

I started finding free tools I had overlooked for years.

I picked up skills I had been paying other people to do — and got better at them than I expected.

I negotiated trades instead of cash payments.

I made "what's in my hand" enough to take the next step.

It wasn't easy.

It wasn't glamorous.

But I learned that forward motion is still possible when your pockets are nearly empty — if you're willing to get resourceful.

PRACTICAL MOVES FOR LOW-RESOURCE SEASONS

When resources run low, don't freeze — get strategic.

1. **Take Inventory** – Write down everything you already have access to: skills, tools, relationships, platforms, spaces, and even your knowledge. You might be sitting on more value than you realize.

2. **Cut the Non-Essentials** – Strip your plan down to the bare minimum actions that directly move the vision forward. If it doesn't produce progress, it doesn't make the cut right now.

3. **Trade Value for Value** – Your skills, services, and connections can be currency. Barter with others who

have what you need. A fair trade can be just as powerful as a cash payment.

4. **Seek Free or Low-Cost Solutions** – There are more free resources available than most people ever tap into. From open-source software to community programs, low-cost doesn't have to mean low-quality.

5. **Stay in Motion** – Progress doesn't always come in big leaps. Even the smallest steps — a phone call, a new skill learned, a single page completed — keep the momentum alive and your vision breathing.

THE FAITH FACTOR

Low-resource seasons are where faith either deepens or dissolves.

It's easy to say you trust God when the account is full, the plan is funded, and everything is in place.

It's another thing entirely when the numbers don't add up, the bills are looming, and you can't see how it's all going to work.

What I've learned is this: God doesn't always send the provision before you move.

Sometimes, **the provision is waiting on the other side of your step.**

Faith in these moments is less about feeling confident and more about moving anyway.

It's showing up with what you have and trusting God to meet you in the gap.

It's refusing to let what's missing dictate whether or not you move forward.

And here's the mystery — over and over, I've seen God provide in motion:

· The door opened when I knocked.
· The help came after I started building.
· The resource showed up once I acted like it was already on the way.

Faith is not just believing God can — it's acting like He will.

A small budget doesn't mean a small destiny.

Too many dreams die because the vision was downsized to match the resources, instead of the strategy being upgraded to match the vision.

This is the proving ground.

If you can keep moving, creating, and building in the lean seasons, you'll have an unstoppable momentum when the overflow comes.

The truth is, overflow exposes the unprepared just as much as scarcity tests the committed.

But when you've been trained by tight seasons, you know how to stretch a dollar, maximize a minute, and make progress without perfect conditions.

So don't pull back — tighten the plan, focus the effort, and keep building.

Because **if you can grow something here, you'll multiply it in the next season**.

* * *

Reflection: Identify one project, goal, or task you've been delaying because you "don't have enough" right now. Write down three things you can do today with the resources you currently have to get it moving.

Declaration: "I am not limited by what I lack. I will use what I have, do what I can, and trust that more will come as I move. I am built to keep moving by any means necessary."

8

THE POWER OF FOCUSED ISOLATION

There's a difference between being alone and being **strategically alone**.

Alone without intention can feel like punishment — a sense of being cut off or forgotten.

But focused isolation? **That's not punishment, that's positioning**.

It's when you decide to step away from the noise, the opinions, and the constant pull of other people's urgency so you can hear your own thoughts and God's voice more clearly.

In a world that thrives on distraction, the ability to withdraw with purpose is a superpower.

It's in these moments — when the notifications are silenced, the calendar is clear, and the door is closed — that you can:

- See the next steps without outside interference.
- Protect fragile ideas until they're strong enough to stand.
- Work without the drain of explaining your every move.

This isn't about cutting people off; it's about cutting off the noise so your focus can be unshakable.

Because clarity doesn't usually come in the crowd — it comes in the quiet.

WHY FOCUSED ISOLATION MATTERS

When you're in the middle of building something that matters, clarity is currency.

But the more people you let into your process, the more that clarity is at risk.

Too many voices — even well-meaning ones — can weigh your vision down.

Everyone will have advice.

Everyone will have a "better way" for you to do it.

Some will offer wisdom.

Others will unknowingly plant doubt.

Focused isolation flips the script.

It puts you back in control of the atmosphere surrounding your vision.

It's where you decide:

- Who gets access to your time.
- Whose feedback actually matters.
- Which voices get a seat at the table — and which don't.

In this space, your vision isn't constantly on trial.

You're not defending it. You're developing it.

It's just you, God, and the select few voices you intentionally choose.

That's not selfish — that's stewardship.

Because **every great work needs a protected season before it's ready for public opinion**.

FOCUSED ISOLATION VS. ACCIDENTAL ISOLATION

Let's be honest — not all isolation is strategic.
Some of it just happens to you.
Accidental isolation shows up when:

- People walk away.
- Support you thought you had disappeared.
- Life shifts, and suddenly you're the only one left holding the vision.

It's not planned — it's survival. And while accidental isolation can still produce growth, it often comes with loneliness, doubt, and frustration.
Focused isolation, though?
That's a decision.
It's when you say:
"I'm stepping back, not because I have to, but because I know I need to."
It's choosing to pull away from:

- The constant updates.
- The endless check-ins.
- The noise of other people's urgency.

Why? Because **not every voice deserves access to your process**, and **not every distraction deserves your time**.
Focused isolation is about shutting distractions out — not

people.

It's about creating an environment where progress isn't interrupted every five minutes by something that doesn't move the needle.

MY ISOLATION SHIFT

I used to believe the only way to stay relevant was to be every-where.

In the mix. At the meetings. On the calls. Showing up to every award show, media events, etc.

If I wasn't seen, I assumed I was falling behind.

But then the vision I was building started demanding more — not more visibility, but more focus.

And I had to face a hard truth:

The more time I gave to people, the less time I gave to progress.

So I pulled back.

- Fewer calls.
- Fewer meetings that went nowhere.
- Fewer social distractions **disguised** as "opportunities."

And in that quiet space?

- Ideas didn't just come — **they flooded in**.
- Plans became sharper.
- **Progress picked up speed**.

I didn't lose relevance. I gained momentum.

THE BENEFITS OF FOCUSED ISOLATION

When you intentionally limit distractions, you create a space where both your work and your spirit can thrive.

1. **Think Deeper** – Without constant interruptions, your mind can move past surface-level thoughts. You begin connecting ideas, identifying patterns, and creating solutions you'd never see in a noisy environment.

2. **Work Faster** – Every unnecessary conversation is time stolen from action. Focused isolation gives you long, uninterrupted stretches to actually do the work — and you'll be shocked how much faster you move when you're not constantly starting and stopping.

3. **Hear God Clearly** – Divine direction often comes in whispers. The more noise you allow in, the harder it is to hear the still, small voice that holds your next instruction. Isolation turns the volume down on the world so you can turn it up on Him.

4. **Protect Your Momentum** – Every opinion carries weight, but not all are worth carrying. In focused isolation, you get to filter which voices are allowed to influence your moves — and you keep your vision on track without being pulled in every direction.

Focused isolation isn't just about getting away from others — it's about getting closer to the clarity, creativity, and conviction you need to build what's next.

HOW TO STEP INTO FOCUSED ISOLATION

Focused isolation doesn't happen by accident — it's a choice you make and a boundary you protect. Here's how to step into it with intention:

1. **Set Clear Boundaries** – Your time is valuable, but only you can enforce it. Let people know when you're unavailable, whether through an auto-reply, calendar blocks, or simply saying, "I'm in a work zone until xyz." Protect your building hours like you would an important meeting — because they are.

2. **Limit Digital Distractions** – Every ping, buzz, and pop-up is a potential derailment. Mute notifications, close extra tabs, and log out of social media during your work blocks. Create an environment where your mind stays locked on the task in front of you.

3. **Create a Dedicated Workspace** – Even if you're working from home, designate a specific area as your "building zone." Physically separating your workspace from your rest space helps train your brain to focus when you enter it — and to release the work when you leave it.

4. **Schedule Connection Intentionally** – Focused isolation isn't about disappearing; it's about making your connections count. Check in with the right people at the right times. Keep your conversations purposeful, your social time replenishing, and your focus uninterrupted.

When you step into focused isolation, you're not cutting the world off — you're tuning the world out so you can tune into the work that matters most.

WHEN ISOLATION FEELS UNCOMFORTABLE

In the beginning, focused isolation can feel unsettling.

The noise quiets.

The constant chatter fades.

And for a moment, you notice the emptiness — not because something's wrong, but because your mind has been trained to crave constant input.

You might find yourself tempted to "check in" with people just to feel connected, even if it means slowing your momentum. But the truth is:

If you can push through that initial discomfort, **the quiet will transform into fuel**.

You'll start hearing your own ideas more clearly.

You'll start recognizing the difference between urgent and important.

And most importantly, you'll start seeing the kind of progress that only happens when distractions are silenced.

Focused isolation is never about cutting yourself off from people forever.

It's about creating a temporary environment where progress has your full attention — so that when you do step back into the crowd, you're walking in with results.

It's the greenhouse where your vision grows before the world ever sees the fruit.

Just like seeds can't thrive in the open air before they've taken root, your ideas need a protected environment to develop.

In a greenhouse, the climate is controlled, the distractions are minimized, and **growth happens quietly** — often unnoticed by anyone outside.

The same is true for your vision.

Focused isolation creates a safe, intentional space where you can water your ideas, prune your plans, and protect them from the premature opinions of others.

When the season shifts and the time is right, what you've been building in private will be strong enough to stand in public.

And by then, **it won't just be an idea — it will be a living, thriving reality, ready to bear fruit**.

* * *

Reflection: What's one distraction you can intentionally remove from your life this week to give your vision more space? Write it down — and commit to acting on it for the next 7 days.

Declaration: "I will protect my vision by limiting my distractions. I choose focused isolation so that my ideas, faith, and momentum can grow. I am built to keep moving by any means necessary."

III

By Any Means Necessary

There comes a point when excuses run out and determination takes over. By any means necessary is more than a phrase — it's a mindset. It means early mornings when you'd rather sleep. Late nights when you'd rather quit. Moving forward even when the money, support, or applause isn't there. It's the grit to say, "If I have to crawl, I'll crawl — but I will not stop." Vision doesn't survive on comfort; it survives on commitment. And that commitment must be relentless.

9

CARRYING YOUR OWN VISION

NO ONE will ever carry your vision with the same weight, urgency, and passion as you.

They might help for a season.

They might cheer from the sidelines.

They might even fight beside you in certain battles.

But the truth is — the vision was given to you, not to them.

It was placed in your spirit, entrusted to your stewardship, and fueled by your unique calling.

Others can assist, but they can't feel the same fire that keeps you awake at night.

They don't carry the same responsibility to protect it when it's fragile, nurture it when it's growing, and defend it when it's attacked.

That's not a burden — it's an assignment.

And assignments come with accountability.

At the end of the day, when the applause fades and the helpers move on, it's your hands that must still be on the plow.

Your consistency will decide whether the vision thrives or dies.

WHY WAITING FOR OTHERS WILL COST YOU

Waiting for someone else to believe in your vision before you act is one of the fastest ways to suffocate momentum.

Here's why:

- **They Can't See What You See** – God didn't give them the blueprint. They weren't in the room when He spoke to you, and they don't carry the mental picture burned into your spirit.

- **They Don't Feel What You Feel** – The weight of urgency, the late-night stirring, the deep conviction — that's tied to your calling, not theirs.

- **They Have Their Own Battles** – Expecting them to put your vision above their own responsibilities will only lead to disappointment.

When you **delay your obedience, waiting for human validation**, you risk **missing the divine timing attached to your assignment**.

God often calls you to move first — before the applause, before the partnership, before the "yes" from anyone else.

Sometimes the most powerful step of faith you can take is the one you take alone.

WHEN I LEARNED THIS LESSON

I used to believe that if I could just get people to see my vision as vividly as I did, they would naturally join me and stay the course.

I thought that passion was magnetic — that once they caught it, they'd never let go.

But reality taught me otherwise. **Even the most enthusiastic supporters can lose momentum when the grind gets real**, when progress slows, or when sacrifices feel too costly.

I remember the day it hit me. I looked around for extra hands to help carry the load... and there was **no one there**.

No cheering section.

No reinforcements.

No safety net.

It was just me, the vision, and God who gave it to me.

And in that moment, something shifted. I realized **this journey isn't defined by who else is willing to carry the weight — it's defined by whether I am willing to carry it no matter who walks away, no matter how heavy it feels, and no matter how long it takes.**

That's when my commitment deepened. Because **vision isn't sustained by agreement — it's sustained by ownership.**

THE MINDSET SHIFT

There's a moment in every builder's journey when you stop looking around for who's going to help and start looking in the mirror.

That's the moment when you accept — **fully, unapologetically** — that **your vision is your responsibility!**

When that realization lands, **everything shifts**.
You stop stalling while waiting for:

· Perfect conditions to fall into place.
· Enough people to "get it" and rally behind you.
· Someone else to step in and carry the heavy end of the load.

Instead, a new set of declarations takes root in your spirit:

· "If it has to be me, **I'll do it!**"
· "If no one else shows up, **I'm still moving!**"
· "If I have to crawl, I'll crawl — but **I will not stop!**"

This is where ownership replaces wishful thinking.
 This is where **determination becomes your default setting**.
 And this is where visions survive the drought seasons —
because you refuse to let them die in your hands.

THE WEIGHT AND THE REWARD

Carrying your own vision will test you in ways nothing else can.
 It's not light.
 It's not convenient.
 And it will not always feel fair.
 Some days it will feel like you're dragging the entire dream
uphill with no one in sight to hand you water.
 You'll work while others rest.
 You'll push while others pull back.
 You'll keep showing up when **NO applause, validation, or
reassurance comes**.
 Truth be told — **that weight is shaping you**.

It's building a resilience you can't buy and a **confidence you can't fake**.

There's a strength in knowing you didn't stop just because the help didn't show up on time.

And the reward? It's twofold:

1. **Internal Victory** – You'll look at what you've built and know, I made it happen with what I had. That's a level of self-trust no one can take away.

2. **External Alignment** – The right help will eventually show up — not because you begged, pleaded, or convinced them, but because your consistency made it undeniable that you're worth standing beside.

The vision becomes magnetic when it's in motion.

And people are drawn to momentum.

PRACTICAL WAYS TO CARRY YOUR VISION WELL

Carrying your vision is part endurance, part strategy.

If you want to do it well — and without burning out — you have to be intentional about how you carry it, not just that you carry it.

1. **Clarify Your Next Step** – Big visions can be paralyzing if you try to tackle them all at once. Instead of obsessing over everything that still needs to be done, identify the single, most important next move. Then take it — and only after that, take the next one. Forward motion is built one step at a time.

2. **Build Systems You Can Manage Alone** – Don't design your workflow around a "team" that doesn't exist yet. Create systems, processes, and habits that work for your current reality. If you get help later, great — but for now, make sure you can keep things moving even if it's just you.

3. **Guard Your Energy** – Carrying a vision is a marathon, not a sprint. That means caring for your body with rest, fuel, and movement; protecting your mind from constant negativity; and keeping your spirit nourished through prayer, worship, and encouragement. You can't pour from an empty cup.

4. **Celebrate Small Wins** – Don't wait until the final vision is complete to acknowledge progress. Every finished task, every breakthrough idea, every step forward deserves recognition. These moments keep your momentum alive when the road feels long.

Carrying your own vision might feel like a burden at first, but over time, it becomes a badge of honor.

In the early days, it can feel overwhelming — the weight of responsibilities, the endless to-do list, the uncertainty of whether you can actually pull it off.

But as you keep going, something shifts.

You begin to see the late nights, the sacrifices, and the moments of doubt as part of your training ground.

Every challenge you've carried through without quitting becomes evidence that you're built for what's ahead.

It's no longer just about the vision itself — it's about the person you've become in the process.

That weight transforms into proof:

- Proof of your commitment.
- Proof of your resilience.
- Proof that you were chosen for this work, and you've been equipped to finish it.

Eventually, you don't just carry the vision — the vision carries you.

* * *

Reflection: What part of your vision have you been waiting for someone else to help you with? Write down one action you can take this week to move it forward yourself.

Declaration: "I will not wait for others to carry what God has given me. I am willing, able, and equipped to carry my vision until it comes to life. I am built to keep moving by any means necessary."

10

BUILT TO KEEP MOVING

Some people are built for comfort.

They thrive in stability, routine, and predictability. Their goal is to avoid disruption and keep life as easy as possible.

Some are built for convenience.

They gravitate toward the path of least resistance, looking for shortcuts and ways to bypass the struggle.

But then there are those of us who are built for movement — the ones who can't sit still when there's work to be done, who feel the pull of destiny even when the path is unclear. We are the ones who keep going:

- Even when it hurts.
- Even when it's lonely.
- Even when every voice inside and outside says, "Stop."

We understand that progress doesn't wait for perfect conditions. We've made peace with discomfort because we know it's part of the journey.

If you're reading this, I believe you're one of those people

— **someone wired for more**, someone who moves forward not because it's easy, but because **stopping isn't an option**.

PROGRESS OVER PITY

When life hits hard, pity can feel like a warm blanket — safe, comforting, and familiar.

It's tempting to stay there, wrapping yourself in the "why me" questions, replaying the hurt, and reliving the unfair moments.

But pity has a dark side.

- Pity never builds.
- Pity never moves.
- Pity keeps you in the same place, rehearsing the problem instead of working toward the solution.

The people who are truly built for movement make a different choice.

They refuse to let temporary pain become a permanent position.

They trade pity for progress.

They say to themselves:

"I may not be where I want to be yet, but I will not still be here a year from now."

"I will not let my story stall here."

"I will take a step — even if it's small — because forward is the only direction I accept."

Progress over pity is not about ignoring your pain — it's about refusing to let it be the reason you stop moving.

IT'S A DECISION, NOT A FEELING

Being built to keep moving has nothing to do with feeling strong all the time.

In fact, most of the time, you won't feel strong at all.

It's about making a choice — a deliberate, stubborn decision — to move when you feel the weakest.

It's about getting up after another "no" tries to knock the wind out of you.

It's about sending the email after the first one went unanswered.

It's about making the call after the last one was ignored.

It's about showing up — again and again — even when everything in you wants to sit down.

Because here's the truth:

Doors don't open for the person who almost showed up. They open for the one who keeps knocking.

The secret is this:

Your feelings don't have to agree for you to take the next step.

You don't have to wait for confidence to take action.

You don't have to wait for motivation to show up before you move.

Action breeds momentum.

Momentum builds faith.

And faith keeps you moving — even when feelings try to hold you still.

MY BREAKING POINT

I've had moments where stopping seemed like the most logical choice.

When the bank account was lower than the bills.

When the people I thought I could count on slipped away quietly.

When I was worn out from being "the strong one" for everyone else.

I've stood at the edge of quitting, looking at the mountain ahead and thinking, What's the point?

And honestly, it would have been easier to sit down right there, to call it enough, to tell myself, I tried.

But every single time I reached that edge, something inside of me refused to let go.

That "something" wasn't pride.

It wasn't even stubbornness.

It was the unshakable awareness that God hadn't brought me through storms, battles, and sleepless nights just to leave me stranded in the middle.

So I kept moving.

Not because the path suddenly got easier.

Not because I magically felt stronger.

But because **stopping would have meant throwing away every tear, every sacrifice, every sleepless night, and every ounce of faith I had already invested**.

And I decided I couldn't live with that.

THE BUILT-TO-MOVE MINDSET

People who are built to keep moving think differently.

They understand that waiting for the "perfect moment" is often just a disguised form of procrastination.

So they start with what they have — the resources on hand, the knowledge they already carry, and the faith that more will come as they go.

They don't see obstacles as proof they should stop; they see them as redirection. A roadblock isn't the end — it's just an invitation to find another way through, around, or over.

They treat momentum like it's sacred. Once they've pushed past the hardest part — **getting started** — they protect that movement fiercely. They don't allow distractions, unnecessary drama, or fear to slow the pace they've worked so hard to build.

And above all, they've mastered the truth that "slow" **progress is still progress**.

They know that inching forward is infinitely better than standing still — because **even a crawl gets you closer to the finish line**.

YOU WERE MADE FOR THIS

If you've survived heartbreak, disappointment, loss, rejection, closed doors, seasons of scarcity — and you're still here — that's not an accident. That's proof.

Proof that you are **built for the fight**.

Proof that you are **built for the climb**.

Proof that you are **built for the breakthrough that's coming**.

It doesn't mean the journey hasn't worn you down at times.

It doesn't mean you haven't cried, questioned, or even wanted to quit.

It doesn't mean you haven't felt the weight of the calling or the pressure of carrying so much on your own.

What it does mean is that **something deep inside of you refuses to die**.

That even in your weakest moments, there's still a flicker — a stubborn ember — that says, "**I can't stop here.**"

It means that no matter how hard it gets... you will find a way to move forward.

Even if it's slow.

Even if it's messy.

Even if all you can do today is take one small, shaky step.

Because you weren't just called to start — you were made to finish.

Life will test you — not once, but over and over.

It will press you to see what you're really made of.

It will throw storms, delays, detours, and disappointments at you, not to destroy you, but to reveal the strength you didn't know you had.

People will doubt you.

Some will underestimate you because **they can't see past your current season**.

Others will project their own fears and limitations onto your vision.

You'll hear "it's not possible" more times than you can count — and sometimes, it'll come from the people you thought would be your biggest supporters.

Circumstances will try to break you.

There will be days when everything seems to hit at once — the finances, the relationships, the opportunities that slip through your fingers.

Moments where quitting will look like the easiest way out.

But here's the thing:

If you refuse to stop — if you keep moving by any means necessary — **no setback can hold you down**.

No scarcity can strip away what's truly yours.

No separation can keep you from the door God already has your name on.

Because what's meant for you will always be bigger than what's against you.

* * *

Reflection: What's one area of your life right now where you've been standing still out of fear, fatigue, or frustration? Write down one small step you can take today to start moving again.

Declaration "I am built to keep moving. I choose progress over pity. I will not stop for obstacles, delays, or disappointments. I will reach what God has for me — by any means necessary."

11

YOUR MOMENTUM IS YOUR MIRACLE

There's something powerful about movement — even the smallest step forward can shift everything around you.

It's almost as if the moment you decide to stop standing still, heaven and earth take notice.

The atmosphere begins to rearrange itself to align with the direction you're headed.

Opportunities you didn't even know existed start showing up.

A random conversation leads to a connection you've been praying for.

Resources you thought were out of reach suddenly become available.

People who carry the wisdom, skills, or influence you need seem to "accidentally" cross your path — but you know it's no accident at all.

And those doors? The ones that felt like they'd been welded shut?

They begin to loosen, creak, and crack open — not because you forced them, but because your movement created the pressure that made them give way.

This isn't coincidence.

This is **the law of momentum at work**.

When you move, you create energy. When you create energy, things in motion are drawn to you.

Movement doesn't just change your location — **it changes what's available to you**.

MOMENTUM FEEDS MIRACLES

Momentum is more than just movement — it's a declaration.

It's you saying, without words, "I'm committed. I'm invested. I'm in this for real."

Momentum is powerful because it proves you believe in what you're building.

It sends a signal to heaven, to the world around you, and even to the deepest parts of yourself: "This matters to me enough to keep going, even without all the answers."

And the fact is — miracles rarely meet you while you're sitting still.

They meet you in motion.

Think about it:

- The widow in the Bible didn't see the oil overflow until **she started pouring what she had left**.
- Peter didn't experience the impossible — walking on water — until **he made the choice to step out of the boat**.
- The man with the withered hand didn't see healing until **he stretched it out**.

In every case, the miracle wasn't waiting at the starting line —

it was waiting along the way.

It showed up after movement, not before.

You won't see your next until you start moving from your now.

The doors you're praying for won't swing open until **you walk toward them**.

The opportunities you're waiting on won't reveal themselves **until you step into their territory**.

Miracles feed on motion.

And when you choose to keep moving, even when it's slow, even when it's uphill, you position yourself to meet your break-through halfway.

MY PROOF OF THIS PRINCIPLE

I've lived this truth enough times to know it**'s not just theory — it's reality**.

I've had seasons where the math didn't make sense.

Where the next bill loomed larger than my bank account.

Where the dream God gave me seemed to cost more than I could ever afford.

In those moments, the temptation was strong to pause... to wait for a perfect sign... to hope for someone else to swoop in with the answer.

But every time I chose to move anyway — to make the call, start the project, release the idea — something shifted.

Sometimes, it was unexpected money showing up right on time.

Other times, it was a divine connection I could've never orchestrated on my own.

And sometimes, it was simply the clarity to see a solution I had been blind to before.

None of those breakthroughs came while I was sitting still, staring at the problem.

They came after I moved.

After I acted in faith.

After I took the step I could take, even when it didn't seem big enough to matter.

It's taught me this:

You don't wait for the stars to align before you start — you start, and then you watch God align the stars.

WHY MOMENTUM WORKS

1. **Movement Builds Faith** – Every step forward, no matter how small, strengthens your belief that the next one is possible. You begin to see evidence that you can do hard things, and that what felt impossible yesterday is within reach today.

2. **Movement Attracts Attention** – The world notices those who are building, not just talking. People are drawn to action-takers. When they see you moving, they're more likely to believe in your vision and want to be a part of it.

3. **Movement Creates Options** – When you're already in motion, new opportunities naturally appear. Doors you didn't even know existed begin to open because you're closer to them than when you were standing still.

4. **Movement Multiplies Resources** – The more you move, the more resourceful you become. You start to see new

ways to stretch what you have, leverage what's available, and unlock what's been hidden. It's like momentum flips a switch that makes you see possibilities you couldn't see before.

BREAKING THE STANDSTILL

If you've been stuck, here's how to kickstart momentum:

- **Start Small** – Don't underestimate the power of tiny wins. Sometimes the act of simply completing one small task is enough to break mental and emotional paralysis. Small steps compound over time.

- **Create Daily Non-Negotiables** – Choose one to three actions that you commit to doing every day, no matter how you feel. These small, consistent moves become the engine that drives your progress forward.

- **Track Your Progress** – Keep a visible record of your wins, no matter how small. Seeing growth — even in inches — keeps you encouraged and reminds you that movement is happening.

- **Say Yes to Aligned Opportunities** – Don't hold out for the "perfect" opportunity. Instead, take advantage of what aligns with your direction right now. Each aligned step is a bridge to the bigger vision.

THE MIRACLE OF MOTION

One of the biggest lies is that you must wait for the miracle before you start moving. The truth? **Movement is often the miracle**.

Every step forward whispers to your future, "I believe enough to act."

It's a declaration to heaven, to the earth, and to yourself that you are serious about what you've been called to do.

Miracles are often attracted to momentum. When you keep moving with that kind of faith — the faith that acts before the answer — the impossible starts to align.

Doors you couldn't have forced open begin to swing wide.

Resources you couldn't have manufactured start showing up.

Connections you never could have orchestrated begin to cross your path.

And you realize... the miracle wasn't just the breakthrough — it was that you moved when it didn't make sense.

Momentum isn't some mysterious, untouchable force — it's proof.

Proof that you're not waiting for someone to come and rescue you.

Proof that you're willing to meet your future halfway, showing up with what you have right now.

Proof that you are built to keep moving, even when the path ahead isn't fully lit and the answers haven't yet arrived.

And here's the beautiful truth: **sometimes, the greatest miracle isn't in what shows up while you're moving — it's in who you become because you kept moving.**

Movement shapes you.

It stretches your faith.

It sharpens your resilience.

It rewrites the story you once believed about your own limitations.

The doors you walk through may be the reward, but the person you've become on the journey? That's the real treasure.

* * *

Reflection: Where in your life have you been waiting for the "miracle" before you move? Write down one thing you can do today to create momentum in that area.

Declaration: "I will not wait for perfect conditions. I will move now, knowing that momentum itself is my miracle. I am built to keep moving by any means necessary."

12

THE BREAKTHROUGH ON THE OTHER SIDE OF GRIT

Grit is the muscle you build when you refuse to quit.

It's the stubborn refusal to bow to setbacks, delays, and disappointments.

It's the choice to keep showing up when it would be easier to stop.

And here's the promise I can make: if you keep moving long enough, you will see the payoff.

BREAKTHROUGH FEELS DIFFERENT WHEN YOU'VE FOUGHT FOR IT

There's a difference between breakthrough handed to you and **breakthrough you've bled for**.

When you've poured in early mornings, late nights, and more "push" than you thought you had...

When you've worked in seasons of separation, scarcity, and silence...

When you've carried the vision without applause or assistance...

The breakthrough doesn't just feel like a win.

It feels like justice.

MY BREAKTHROUGH MOMENT

I remember a season when I had been grinding for what felt like forever without seeing much return.

I was tired — not just in my body, but deep in my spirit.

I had been showing up day after day, doing the work, and wondering if anything was actually moving.

Then one day, the call came.

The opportunity I had been believing for — the one that had seemed impossible — opened up.

The door that had been locked for years didn't just crack... it swung wide open.

And in that moment, the weight I had been carrying for so long suddenly felt light.

Every sleepless night, every sacrifice, every tear I had pushed past — it all made sense.

It wasn't random.

It wasn't luck.

It was harvest.

Harvest from seeds I'd planted when no one was watching.

Harvest from prayers I had whispered when I didn't even know if I had the strength to keep believing.

Harvest from steps I took in faith when I didn't have a guarantee of the outcome.

And that's the thing about breakthrough — it rarely comes when it's convenient.

It comes when your faith has been tested, when your patience

**has been stretched, and when your persistence has proven
you're ready for it.**

WHY GRIT PRODUCES BREAKTHROUGH

1. **Consistency Creates Opportunity** – Every time you show
   up, you give heaven and earth another chance to align for
   you. Opportunities rarely land in the laps of those who stop
   showing up. They find the ones still moving, still building,
   still believing.

2. **Pressure Sharpens Skill** – The very challenges you wish
   would go away are often the training ground for your next
   level. Every obstacle forces you to think differently, act
   smarter, and strengthen your resolve. The fight is the
   forge that prepares you for what you've been asking for.

3. **Faith in Action Moves Mountains** – Breakthrough doesn't
   just respond to words — it responds to movement. It often
   comes when you've taken steps without any visible sign
   that they'll work. That's the kind of faith that gets God's
   attention and makes the impossible bow.

HOLDING ON UNTIL IT HAPPENS

The breakthrough you've been praying, working, and believing
for often shows up right after the moment you feel like quitting.

That's not an accident. The closer you get to the finish line,
the more resistance you'll feel. The enemy knows he can't stop
what God has already ordained — but if he can get you to stop
yourself, he wins without a fight.

So the pressure increases. Doubt whispers louder. Unexpected roadblocks pop up. The vision starts feeling heavier than the hope that started it.

This is where grit becomes your lifeline. Not because it makes the road smooth — but because it keeps you moving when every sign around you says, "It's not worth it."

Breakthrough isn't always about speed. It's about staying in the fight long enough to see the door swing open, the opportunity arrive, and the promise manifest.

If you can hold on past the urge to quit, you'll discover something amazing — **it was closer than you thought the whole time.**

LIVING IN THE OVERFLOW

When breakthrough finally comes, you realize it's so much bigger than the one thing you were chasing. Yes, the goal is important. Yes, the answered prayer matters. But standing on the other side, you begin to see clearly — it wasn't just about getting something.

It was about becoming someone.

Because somewhere between the fight and the finish line... you became:

- **Stronger** — able to carry more than you thought possible.

- **Wiser** — equipped with insight you couldn't have learned any other way.

- **Unshakable** — rooted so deeply that no storm can uproot you again.

And then you realize something even more powerful: the breakthrough wasn't the final prize — you were.

You are the living proof that persistence pays off. That faith under fire still works. That momentum, once guarded and nurtured, will take you farther than you dreamed.

This is the overflow — not just blessings you can touch, but the strength, clarity, and courage you now carry within you. And from here on out, you move differently... because you know you were **built to keep moving**.

* * *

Reflections: Think of one area in your life where you feel like you're close to giving up. Ask yourself: If my breakthrough was one more step away, would I quit now? Write down one thing you will do to keep going this week.

Declaration: "I will not quit before I reach my breakthrough. My grit is greater than my doubt, my faith is stronger than my fear, and my determination will carry me into overflow. I am built to keep moving by any means necessary."

Afterword

BY ANY MEANS NECESSARY

If you've made it this far, then you've walked with me through more than just words on a page. You've traveled through the quiet seasons where nothing seemed to move. You've felt the sting of lonely nights where your own thoughts were your only company. You've stretched resources until they could stretch no more. You've carried loads so heavy that they made your back ache and your spirit weary.

You've been there when people walked away. You've had plans that seemed unshakable crumble to dust in your hands. You've had to start over — not once, but more times than you ever imagined. And you've heard that voice deep inside whisper, "This is too much. Maybe it's time to let go."

But here's the part that matters most: you didn't.

Because here you are.

Still standing.

Still breathing.

Still holding the vision in your heart like a sacred treasure.

You may be bruised, but you are not broken. You may be tired, but you are not finished. And no matter what it took to get here, you've proven something unshakable — you were built for this.

THIS BOOK WASN'T JUST A STORY — IT WAS A MIRROR

What you've been holding in your hands wasn't just a collection of my moments, my memories, or my milestones. Every page you've read was also a reflection of you — your battles, your valleys, your quiet victories. It wasn't written so you could admire my journey, but so you could recognize your own.

Truth is, you are not weak for feeling the weight. You are human.

You are not broken because the road has been rough. You are being built in the fire.

If anything, this journey should have reminded you of one thing above all: you are still here for a reason. Not by accident. Not by coincidence. But because something in you was designed to keep moving, no matter the resistance.

And if you've made it this far, then you already carry the proof.

You were built for this.

You were made to endure.

You were never meant to quit.

THE REAL WIN

The victory isn't just in the final outcome — it's in the fact that you made it through the middle. That messy, lonely, uncertain space where most people give up... but you didn't.

The real win is that you proved to yourself you can move without waiting for permission. You can make progress without needing a crowd to clap for you. You can push forward without the luxury of perfect conditions.

You've discovered along the way that:

- **Separation is preparation** — sometimes God will pull you apart from the familiar so He can pull you into the future.

- **Scarcity breeds creativity** — lack didn't kill you; it sharpened your resourcefulness.

- **Grit opens the door to breakthrough** — it's not the gift that gets you there, it's the grind.

- **Momentum attracts miracles** — once you move, heaven moves with you.

But the most important truth you've uncovered?

You already have what it takes to finish what you've started. You're not "becoming" ready — you are ready.

YOUR TURN

I've carried my vision by any means necessary — now it's your turn.

Don't just close this book and drift back into "normal." Normal is comfortable, but it's also the graveyard of dreams. Decide — right now — that this is the season you stop waiting.

No more waiting for perfect timing — because perfect timing is a myth.

No more waiting for everyone to "get it" — because visionaries are rarely understood in the beginning.

No more waiting for every resource to be neatly stacked in place — because God's provision is often unlocked in the motion, not the pause.

Move with what you have — even if it feels small.

Move with who you are — even if you don't feel "enough" yet.

Move with the God who gave you the vision — because if He planted it, He will grow it.

Your turn has already started. Your yes is the trigger. Your motion is the signal. Your faith in action is the proof.

Because the truth is, you will never regret moving forward — even if it's slow, even if it's messy, even if you have to figure it out as you go. Forward motion leaves you with lessons, growth, and proof that you didn't quit on yourself.

But you will always carry the sting of the moment you stopped short — the "what if" that lingers, the vision that stayed buried, the story that never got finished.

So choose motion over regret.

Choose progress over perfection.

Choose to keep moving until the vision God gave you becomes the reality you're living in.

FINAL DECLARATION

"I will not stop until I see what I've been believing for. I will carry my vision, protect my momentum, and fight for my future by any means necessary. I am built to keep moving — and I will."

Declarations for the Determined

Speak these every day until they become your reality.

1. I am built to keep moving, no matter what comes against me.
2. I choose progress over pity in every situation.
3. I am equipped to carry my vision without waiting for permission.
4. Every setback is a setup for my next level.
5. I will use what I have until I have what I need.
6. Separation will not break me — it will build me.
7. I am disciplined enough to show up when others won't.
8. Scarcity sharpens my creativity and fuels my resourcefulness.
9. My momentum is my miracle, and I protect it daily.
10. I will not quit one step away from my breakthrough.
11. I am strong enough to start over and wise enough to do it better.
12. I turn letdowns into lessons and lessons into action.
13. I will not be distracted by voices that don't carry my vision.
14. I rise early, stay late, and do the work necessary to win.
15. I am relentless in pursuit of what God has placed in my hands.
16. No obstacle is greater than my determination to move

forward.

17. **I trust God's timing, but I move in God's momentum.**
18. **Every day I act, I get closer to what I've been believing for.**
19. **I am unshakable, unbreakable, and unstoppable.**
20. **I am built to keep moving — by any means necessary.**

* * *

Daily Reminder

"No matter what comes against me — people leaving, resources running low, or obstacles rising — I will keep moving forward. I am built for this. I am built to win. I am built to keep moving — by any means necessary."

www.ingramcontent.com/pod-product-compliance
Lightning Source LLC
Chambersburg PA
CBHW071533120626
46550CB00006B/2443

* 9 7 8 1 9 6 9 8 8 3 0 0 2 *